HAUNTED ART

by Elizabeth Andrews

abdobooks.com

Published by Pop!, a division of ABDO, PO Box 398166, Minneapolis, Minnesota 55439. Copyright © 2022 by Abdo Consulting Group, Inc. International copyrights reserved in all countries. No part of this book may be reproduced in any form without written permission from the publisher. DiscoverRoo™ is a trademark and logo of Pop!.

Printed in the United States of America, North Mankato, Minnesota.

102021
012022

THIS BOOK CONTAINS RECYCLED MATERIALS

Cover Photos: Shutterstock Images (photo and pattern)
Interior Photos: Shutterstock Images, 1, 5, 6, 18–19, 21, 22; Gianni Dagli Orti/Shutterstock, 9; Historia/Shutterstock, 10; Werner Forman Archive/Shutterstock, 12; David/Washington, DC/flickr, 17; Alan Wilson/Alamy Stock Photo, 25; Shutterstock, 27, 28

Editor: Tyler Gieseke
Series Designer: Laura Graphenteen

Library of Congress Control Number: 2021943404
Publisher's Cataloging-in-Publication Data

Names: Andrews, Elizabeth, author.
Title: Haunted art / by Elizabeth Andrews
Description: Minneapolis, Minnesota : Pop!, 2022 | Series: Hauntings | Includes online resources and index.
Identifiers: ISBN 9781098241216 (lib. bdg.) | ISBN 9781644946749 (pbk.) | ISBN 9781098241919 (ebook)
Subjects: LCSH: Art--Juvenile literature. | Ghosts--Juvenile literature. | Spirits--Juvenile literature. | Ghost Stories--Juvenile literature.
Classification: DDC 133.1--dc23

WELCOME TO DiscoverRoo!

Pop open this book and you'll find QR codes loaded with information, so you can learn even more!

Scan this code* and others like it while you read, or visit the website below to make this book pop!

popbooksonline.com/haunted-art

*Scanning QR codes requires a web-enabled smart device with a QR code reader app and a camera.

TABLE OF
CONTENTS

CHAPTER 1

THE ART OF THE SCARE

A cursed piece of art seems spookier than other haunted objects. Art is meant to be enjoyed by those who view it. But when the art brings bad fortune, what is

WATCH A VIDEO HERE!

There are many different kinds of art. The materials or methods an artist uses to create a work is called a medium.

one to do? Often, the response is to get rid of the art. Sell it. Hide it. Throw it away. But of course, haunted things never stay gone for long.

Museums are good places to go if you're looking for art with a spooky history.

Pieces of art can become haunted for many reasons. A tortured artist's energy could have transferred to their creation. Maybe a painting was hung on the wall of a room where a terrible death occurred. A statue might even have been stolen from its homeland!

No matter how the art becomes haunted, one thing is certain: it has the power to change people's lives forever.

CHAPTER 2

SET IN STONE

A squat, three-inch (7.6 cm) figure named Little Mannie was known for causing **mischief** in Manchester, England. He was dug up in the 1960s in the basement of a **political** club. A woman named Lucy was cleaning the dirt floors when she thought she saw something.

LEARN MORE HERE!

Stone is a popular medium to make statues with.

Political clubs were often made up of rich people. Members gathered to talk about the world. They would meet in places like libraries, game rooms, and meeting rooms.

People got excited when they learned about Little Mannie. A history professor organized a dig in the basement to see what else they could find. Sure enough, there was more! The **artifacts** in the ground were laid out in a **ritualistic** way, with candles and animal bones. Whoever put the artifacts together was blessing the house.

At first, Lucy didn't want to give

Mannie up to the Manchester Museum.

But soon, bad luck started following her

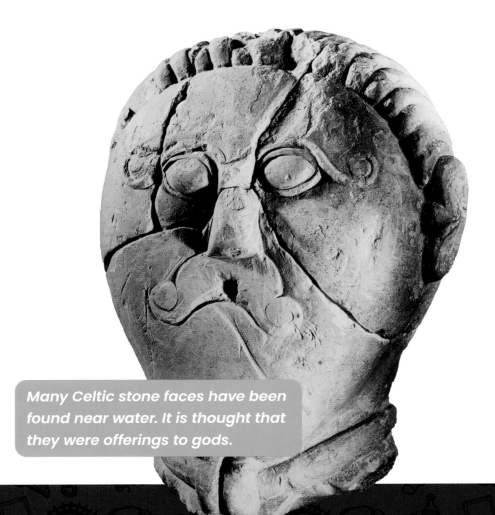

Many Celtic stone faces have been found near water. It is thought that they were offerings to gods.

and her family. She finally handed it over. Then museum employees started suffering **misfortunes** like broken bones and car accidents. Everyone began keeping their distance from Little Mannie.

The history professor assumed Little Mannie was a **Celtic** statue. There were many small, round faces carved into stones found around England. These were made by the Celts. But Mannie was different. He wasn't just a face. He had a whole body.

An expert on African artifacts toured the museum in 1974. He noticed Little Mannie. He knew immediately that Mannie wasn't Celtic. He was from an ancient civilization in Sierra Leone. Mannie, like many other African artifacts, was stolen during British **colonization**. Little Mannie did not like that people took him from his home. And he let people know it!

LITTLE MANNIE

A woman named Pat Ellison-Reed wrapped some of her hair around Little Mannie. She did this to try to magically stop him from causing more trouble.

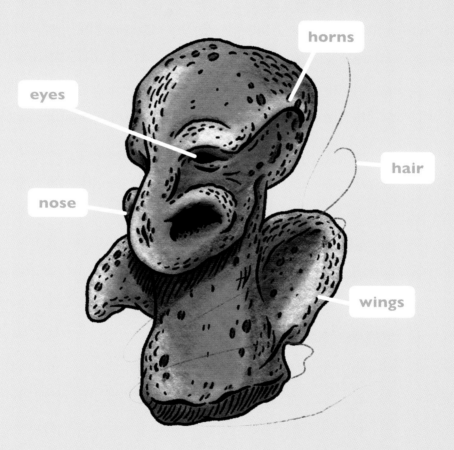

horns

eyes

hair

nose

wings

Statues like Little Mannie were used by the Mende people of Sierra Leone to bless their homes and crops.

CHAPTER 3

A CURSED COPY

In another case of stolen art, Black Aggie looks darkly over all who encounter her. However, her story is more complicated than just being taken from her homeland.

COMPLETE AN ACTIVITY HERE!

Black Aggie is a cast bronze metal sculpture.

Many statues in cemeteries are angels. They are thought to carry the souls of the dead to the afterlife.

Black Aggie once sat in the Druid Ridge **Cemetery** in Maryland. She marked the resting place of **Civil War** officer Felix Agnus and his family. Agnus was a French man who moved to the United States and fought bravely for the Union.

DID YOU KNOW?

People said Felix Agnus had so many small pieces of metal stuck in his body from war injuries, that he rattled when he walked.

After buying land in the Druid Ridge Cemetery, Agnus immediately wanted to decorate it with a funeral sculpture. The artist he hired to create it lied to him.

The artist said he had permission to replicate the famous Adams Memorial. This statue of a sad woman stood guard over Clover Adams's grave. Clover was related to US president John Adams. The memorial artist said no one could ever remake it.

When Agnus's statue was put up, the original artist's wife demanded he take

John Adams was the second president of the United States. His son, John Quincy Adams, was the sixth.

it down. But Agnus did not listen. Instead,

he buried his mother directly beneath it.

When he passed away in 1925, he was

buried beside it.

The large piece of cloth the statue is wearing is called a shroud.

Quickly, stories started spreading around town about the odd sculpture in the cemetery. No grass would ever grow in her shadow. People said her eyes would glow red at night. If you looked into them, you would go blind! Sitting in the statue's lap would curse you.

People also said the cemetery's spirits would gather at the statue once a year! All these happenings are thought to be a product of her creator's actions.

FUNERAL ART

Funeral art has been around since ancient times. People decorate graves with it to show off how much power the deceased had in life. The ancient Egyptians marked the graves of their leaders with giant tombs like the Great Pyramid. They were filled with art. Today, graves marked with sculptures of angels most likely came from families with a lot of money.

CHAPTER 4

UP IN FLAMES

The Crying Boy paintings are creepy enough on their own. Mix in a history of hauntings, and they are terrifying. A European painter put together the series of art. However, he didn't use his real name when he signed his work. The series

LEARN MORE HERE!

Not all paintings in the series show the same boy.

claimed by no one features paintings

of children with tears streaming down

their faces.

The Crying Boy paintings have been **mass-produced** since their creation. This means there are thousands of copies in the world. Attached to all of them is a thrilling legend that began in the 1970s. That's not a very long time ago compared to other hauntings. Still, the paintings are already related to a long list of spooky events.

The paintings first made headlines in England in 1985. A home had suddenly caught fire. Everything was destroyed except for a framed copy

People brought their paintings to be burned at large gatherings. They didn't want to have a cursed piece of art in their home.

of *The Crying Boy*. A firefighter noticed this and added to the mystery. He said this wasn't the first time he'd seen an undamaged *Crying Boy* lying in the wreckage of a home fire. In fact, the fire department had fifty examples of copies of this painting surviving fires.

Men pose with their crying boy painting before they destroy it.

Legend says the original subject for *The Crying Boy* paintings was a child named Don Bonillo. He killed his parents in a fire and went on to live a terribly sad life. Perhaps it's his spirit living in every copy of the paintings. He continues to cause the same suffering to the owners that he did his parents.

DID YOU KNOW?

A comedian filmed a video of himself trying to set a copy of *The Crying Boy* on fire. Only a small corner burned. Nothing else.

MAKING CONNECTIONS

TEXT-TO-SELF

Which piece of haunted art did you find most spooky? Why?

TEXT-TO-TEXT

Have you read any other books about hauntings or ghosts? What did they have in common with these stories?

TEXT-TO-WORLD

Do you think people should take art from its original home? Explain why or why not.

artifact — an object made by humans long ago.

Celt — a person who lived about 2,000 years ago in many countries of western Europe.

cemetery — a place where the dead are buried.

colonization — when one country takes control over the people and land of another country.

mass-produce — to make a lot of something with machines.

mischief — activity that causes annoyance or trouble.

misfortune — an event of bad luck.

political — relating to the government.

ritual — a set form or order to a ceremony.

INDEX

ONLINE RESOURCES
popbooksonline.com

Scan this code* and others like it while you read, or visit the website below to make this book pop!

popbooksonline.com/haunted-art

*Scanning QR codes requires a web-enabled smart device with a QR code reader app and a camera.